Vol. LVII, No. 2   WASHINGTON

THE NATIONAL GEOGRAPHIC MAGAZINE

SEEKING THE MOUNTAINS OF MYSTERY

An Expedition on the China-Tibet Frontier to the Unexplored Amnyi Machen Range, One of Whose Peaks Rivals Everest

BY JOSEPH F. ROCK

Leader of the National Geographic Society Yunnan Expedition, 1927-1930

AUTHOR OF "LIFE AMONG THE LAMAS OF CHONI," "THROUGH THE GREAT RIVER TRENCHES OF ASIA," "THE LAND OF THE YELLOW LAMA," ETC, IN THE NATIONAL GEOGRAPHIC MAGAZINE

With Illustrations from Photographs by the Author

"TO-DAY the map has no more secrets " Idle minds repeat that parrot phrase. But who knows all Tibet, or its far-away frontiers on western China? Even its own prayer-muttering tribes know only their own bleak, wind-swept valleys.

After dangerous, difficult months, I reached the headwaters of the 2,000-mile-long Yellow River and the towering, unexplored range of the Amnyi Machen Twenty-eight thousand feet, or almost as high as Everest, its tallest peak lifts its snow-white head, majestic as the Matterhorn. Here, in remote, almost inaccessible valleys, I found countless wild animals still unafraid of man, peaceful as in Eden Through deep, tree-lined chasms roared the upper reaches of the mighty Yellow River, flowing here *at an elevation of 10,000 feet above the sea !* Here, in July, was ice, and flowers bloomed in the snow.

WORLD MAP SECRETS ON THE CHINA-TIBET FRONTIER

And time turns back a thousand years when one talks to the superstitious and vexatiously inquisitive, suspicious folk who inhabit this lonely nook of the world.

"The earth is flat," they say. "In its middle stands a big mountain. The sun sets by going behind this.

"In far-away lands, men fly, we have heard But in big eagles ; if not in eagles, then in something that must be covered with eagle feathers. And in other lands there are men with the heads of dogs, of yaks and other beasts "

A miserable land it is, of poverty and incredible filth ; a land cut off from all the modern world ; a region which, for uncounted centuries, has had its own forms of government, of religion and social customs, yet a region which knows no railway, no motor car, no radio, or aught of all that science and invention have given the world since Marco Polo's day.

THE FIRST WHITE MAN TO APPROACH THE AMNYI MACHEN FROM THE EAST

Into this region no Chinese dares venture Ninety thousand or more of the warlike Ngoloks live here, and other tribes of Tibetans, with whom they quarrel and fight. Yet of these local wars, not even an echo ever reaches the outside world. Here I saw men with spears 30 feet long, and a room in a lamasery wherein more than

MEMBERS OF THE EXPEDITION NEAR CHONI, IN KANSU PROVINCE

Some of Dr. Rock's Nashi assistants, who accompanied him from Yünnan overland to the Yellow River at Radja, and to the Richthofen Range and borders of the extreme southwest of Mongolia.

A DEVOUT TIBETAN WHIRLS A DOUBLE PRAYER WHEEL

The smaller upper wheel, of silver, revolves separately from the lower; but each contains a roll of paper on which is printed the standard formula, "Om mani padme hum." Each time either wheel revolves the Tibetan is credited with a prayer, according to his belief. This man is a Drokwa, or nomad Tibetan.

A VENERABLE MOSLEM OF OLD TAOCHOW

He belongs to the New Sect, or Sin Chiao, that believes in a savior who lives in Old Taochow and who is known as Jesus or Aissa. The sect also believes in reincarnation. These Mohammedans trade exclusively with the Tibetan nomads, selling brass and copper caldrons, pots, kettles, and barley, taking in exchange wool, furs, and musk.

NOMAD PILGRIM WOMEN AT ANGKUR LAMASERY, IN CHONI

These Tibetan women, with rosaries and prayer wheels, are from the grass lands. They were blessed by the Labrang Buddha, who had fled to Angkur Lamasery during the Tibetan-Mohammedan war (see text, page 140).

50 imported clocks were ticking, no two keeping the same time! No, our world map is not yet without its secrets.

The great Amnyi Machen Range is shown on modern charts of Asia, though it is usually incorrectly spelled Amne Ma-chin. It lies west of the great bend of the Yellow River (Hwang Ho) within the Koko Nor territory, something more than 1,300 miles westerly from Shanghai and 1,200 miles in a northerly direction from Rangoon. It is this range which forces the Yellow River to describe such a large bend (see map, pages 138-9).

Except for occasional wandering missionaries, no whites ever make this hard, perilous journey to the Chino-Tibet frontier. The Russian explorer Roborovski, in the winter of 1895, tried to reach the Amnyi Machen, but was attacked at a spot northeast of the Mangun Pass and driven back by the "Tanguts," the Mongolian name for Tibetans.

My own visit, what from extraordinary hardship and the perils of bandits, was so brief that I could make only limited observations. So, as yet, the world knows only from hearsay of all the Amnyi Machen's mysterious valleys, its lawless Ngolok tribes, and the queen who was supposed to rule over them.

That it fell to my lot to reach this forbidden stronghold of the Ngoloks was due to a chance encounter, back in 1923, with that famous British explorer, Gen. George Pereira. On my way from Burma to southeast Tibet, as leader of an expedition for the National Geographic Society, I met the English traveler at Tengyueh, in Yünnan. He had then recently completed his now historic march from Peking (Peiping) to Lhasa, and, during our visit, he told me of an amazing landmark passed on his westward journey—the great snow-capped Amnyi Machen Range, which he saw from a distance of more than 100 miles.

Very likely, he remarked, the Amnyi Machen, when surveyed, might prove higher than Mount Everest. He also spoke of the turbulent Ngolok tribes and their queen, and of his own ambition to attempt a journey of exploration to their country.

But God disposes. General Pereira died

THE GREAT LABRANG BUDDHA'S PRIVATE CHAPEL.

The *Dju Kung*, or Lord's House, affords an impressive example of sumptuous temple decoration. The garlands hung on strings before the altar are from seeds of *Oroxylum indicum*, the East Indian trumpetflower.

THE NORTHEASTERN END OF LABRANG MONASTERY

The religious community is surrounded by low, narrow sheds containing prayer wheels made of yak hide, gilded and painted with the sacred formula "Om mani padme hum." The lamasery houses nearly 5,000 monks (see, also, text, page 145).

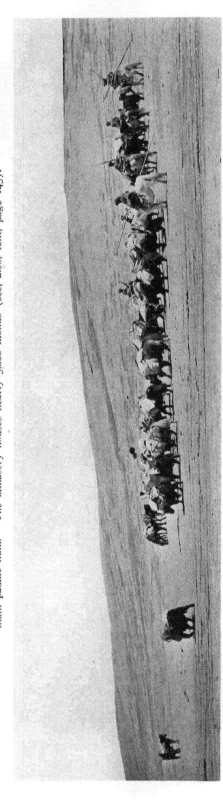

AT HIGH ALTITUDES THE CHINA-TIBET FRONTIER IS A COLD AND EMPTY COUNTRY

Filing through Shawo Valley in the month of May, the author's yak caravan marched at an elevation of 11,500 feet. This point was reached six days west of Labrang, on the trip to Radja.

A PUBLIC MARKET BEFORE THE LABRANG MONASTERY

Venders display their wares in small wooden booths, which are stored in the near-by lamasery when not in use. The bleak nature of the region is indicated by empty hills in the background.

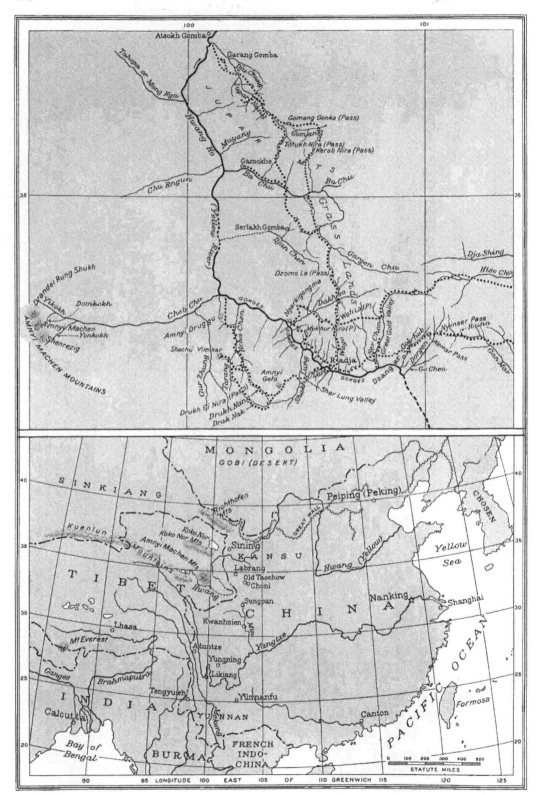

FROM CHONI THE AUTHOR TRAVELED WESTWARD TOWARD THE AMNYI MACHEN
AS FAR AS SHACHÜ YIMKAR:

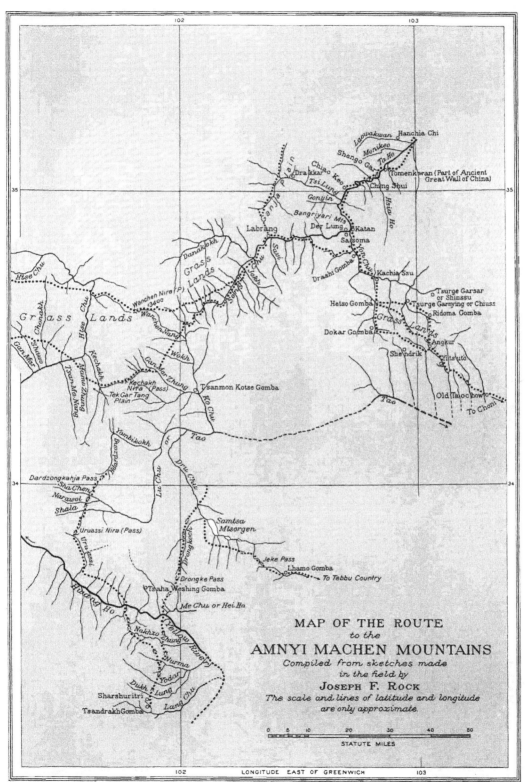

MAP OF THE ROUTE
to the
AMNYI MACHEN MOUNTAINS
Compiled from sketches made
in the field by
JOSEPH F. ROCK
The scale and lines of latitude and longitude
are only approximate.

STATUTE MILES

LONGITUDE EAST OF GREENWICH

Drawn by A. H. Bumstead

ROUTES TO THE SOUTHEAST INDICATE SIDE EXCURSIONS MADE BY DR. ROCK, TO
BE DESCRIBED SUBSEQUENTLY

THREE LABRANG GIRLS OF THE LHARDI TRIBE

Worked into their odd and cumbrous hairdress are ornamental disks of brass sewn on bright-red strips of cloth. One of the girls wears a large sea shell.

all of a previous far journey into China.*

As a base, I first chose Sining, in north-west Kansu. However, after more than 15 weeks of weary marching and casual games of "I spy" with pursuing bandits, we reached the town of Choni and decided to make our base there. It was now late in April.

The best way to reach Amnyi Machen, said the Choni people, was to go by way of the grass lands to Radja Gomba, on the east bank of the Yellow River. But it was easier to hear *how* to go than it was to go. And many a prayer wheel was to rattle and whirl, and much muddy water run down the old Yellow River, before my eyes were to rest on the chaste white peaks of Amnyi Machen.

AN AUDIENCE WITH A BOY BUDDHA

Prince Yang Chi-Ching of Choni, a feudal stay-at-home,

soon afterward on the cold and hostile Chino-Tibet frontier, at almost the end of his third extraordinary overland journey across China.

But it was his passing glimpse of faraway Amnyi Machen and his talk of its unsolved riddles that inspired me to see for myself, if humanly possible, something of its mysteries and magnificence.

Many months later, back in China now for the Arnold Arboretum of Harvard University, I found myself on a botanical and ornithological expedition, with authority to explore, if I could, the Amnyi Machen Range. From Yünnanfu I started with 12 faithful Nashi helpers, veterans

could help me not at all.† However, he was moved to mention the great Living Buddha of Labrang Monastery, the incarnation of the God of Learning, at the moment sheltered in the small monastery of Angkur Gomba, on the Prince's domain. Thither I went, after obtaining a letter of introduction. Angkur Gomba nestled at the foot of a limestone cliff in a narrow valley.

* See, also, "Banishing the Devil of Disease Among the Nashi," by Joseph F. Rock, in the NATIONAL GEOGRAPHIC MAGAZINE for November, 1924.

† See, also, "Life Among the Lamas of Choni," by Joseph F. Rock, in the NATIONAL GEOGRAPHIC MAGAZINE for November, 1928.

I learned that the 12 - year - old Living Buddha had retired to this place because of a war raging between his people about La-brang and the Mos-lems of Sining, led by General Ma Chi, ruler of the Koko Nor country.

But, insignificant as Angkur Gomba itself was, one quickly dis-cerned that it now sheltered an important personage. From the quarters assigned us, in one end of the lamasery, we could see over the walls and ob-serve the motley con-course of people doing obeisance to the Liv-ing Buddha. An un-broken line of grass-land nomads — men, women, and chil-dren—moved around the lamasery, making prostrations or turn-ing prayer wheels and muttering the eternal monotonous phrase, "Om mani padme hum" (O, the Jewel in the Lotus, Amen).

Under a shed near our quarters were suspended hundreds of yak and mutton

THE LIVING BUDDHA OF DZANGAR MONASTERY IS EIGHTY-ONE YEARS OLD

Seated before his Mongol tent, the Buddha is attended by two monks and a boy Buddha. He is garbed in red and yellow and wears a miter on his head.

shoulder blades with prayers printed on them. After the pilgrims had made their cash offerings to the boy Buddha and been blessed, they crowded into this shed to rattle these dry, printed bones. A quick, easy way to pray! This ritual of bone-rattling, with the noise of trumpets, cym-bals, and conches, filled the air as we went to our audience with the Buddha.

Enthroned on the dais, clad in yellow satins and with the miter of a Living Buddha on his brow, sat the boy god. As we came in he arose slowly and bowed. I presented him with the usual *kattak*, or silk scarf, while one of my men lifted up

a tray of presents, which was accepted for the Buddha by an attendant lama. My cook, knowing the required Tibetan dia-lect, acted as interpreter. Through him I explained to the boy Buddha, or rather to his father, who waited on him, my reasons for wishing to explore the Amnyi Machen, and requested a letter to the Buddha of Radja and also letters to some of the Ngolok chiefs.

I readily got the letter to the Buddha of Radja Gomba, but some weeks were to elapse and a bloody war was to be fought between the nomad Tibetans and the Moslems of Sining before I obtained

TIBETAN NOMADS CARRY SWORDS AND RIFLES

On their rifles members of the Sokwo Arik tribe fasten wooden prongs, on which they rest the weapons when firing. They never fire a rifle without using such a rest.

A PORTABLE TALKING MACHINE AMAZED AND DELIGHTED THE TIBETANS

Nomads of the Sokwo Arik (Tibetan) tribe are listening to the Caruso record, "La Donna è Mobile," at the author's camp in the grass lands of the Sokwo Arik winter quarters, four days west of Labrang. The natives called the phonograph a Russian magic box.

my letters to the Ngo-lok chiefs.

To give the reader a more graphic picture of how precarious life is in these wilds, let me hastily sketch some aspects of the w a r which interrupted my progress toward the Amnyi Machen.

A SLAUGHTER RECALL-ING THE DAYS OF GENGHIS KHAN

W h e n the fight started, the Tibetans took the offensive and drove t h e Moslems out of Labrang; but soon the latter re-turned w i t h reën-forcements a n d de-feated the Tibetans in fierce battles fought on the Ganja Plain and in S o n g C h u V a l l e y . In these frightful slaughters, however, the w i l d Ngura, nomad Tibet-ans, made a most dra-matic showing; they charged against the Moslems at full speed on horseback, impal-ing them on their 30-foot lances like men spearing frogs. Far more Moslems were killed with these spears than with guns.

THE SON OF ARIK JOJORO, SOKWO ARIK NOMAD CHIEF, REVEALS NEGROID FEATURES

He wears a single sheepskin garment. About his neck is a rosary bearing a silver talismanic box.

Under any skilled leader the Tibetans could have whipped the Moslems; but there was no coördination among these wild tribes. In fact, during the fight, the Amchoks, although fighting with the Tibet-ans, took advantage of the battle's con-fusion to sneak back and rob the tents of their own allies.

Many of the Tibetans who fell alive into enemy clutches were hung up by their thumbs, disemboweled alive and their ab-dominal cavities were then filled with hot stones.

The Kansu Government troops had promised to help the Tibetans, but they seemed to have no stomach for all this slaughter; anyway, they failed to appear. Finally, despite fierce resistance by the brave but unorganized tribes, the better-trained Moslems routed them completely. Labrang remained in Mohammedan hands. Hetso monastery was plundered and a Living Buddha with 15 monks was slain. Raiding the grass lands, the Moslems had slaughtered women and children as in the ruthless days of Genghis Khan.

TIBETAN HEADS DECORATED GARRISON WALLS

Frightful, indeed, was the aspect of La-brang after the fight. One hundred fifty-

A BUDDHA'S STEWARD GAVE A TEA FOR THE AUTHOR IN THIS TENT

Because of the extremely unsanitary nomad tent life, official teas in Tibet are an ordeal to the rare visiting foreigners (see, also, text, page 152).

four Tibetan heads were strung about the walls of the Moslem garrison like a garland of flowers. Heads of young girls and children decorated posts in front of the barracks. The Moslem riders galloped about the town, each with 10 or 15 human heads tied to his saddle. Heavy tread the heels of the Kansu Mohammedans on these nomad people of Tibet.

Amid this carnage we were forced to give up for the time being any hopes of marching on to our difficult goal.

Glad to escape from a stricken land, I marched my little band north to camp and explore during the rest of the summer in and around the great Koko Nor and in the Richthofen Range. That journey is another story. Late in the fall we returned to Choni to winter. Here, during the long months, I talked with the lamas, attended their ritual dances and festivals, took many photographs with the help of Prince Yang, and gathered all the information I could about the Ngoloks. In the meantime, from the boy Buddha of Labrang I had obtained letters of introduction to the leading Ngolok chiefs, those ruling over the im-

portant Rimong, Kangsar, and Kanggan tribes, who have their camps west of the Yellow River and south and west of the Amnyi Machen Range.

THE START FOR THE AMNYI MACHEN

It was late in the spring, almost a year and a half after my start from America, when I was again ready to press on toward the mountains of mystery.

When we left Choni, we had supplies for a five months' march, including food, a photographic outfit, cotton for stuffing any birds collected, grass paper for packing plant specimens, powdered charcoal for packing seeds; also beans for horse feed and many presents for the important people we were to meet. As coined money is unknown in this part of the world, we carried much lump silver, cotton drill, sateen and other cloth, as well as needles and thread for use in barter.

Dressed in gray felt raincoats, well armed, and escorted by a cavalry guard, we made an imposing party as we marched out of the gates of Choni. We used yak carts to haul our supplies as far as the

THE LIVING BUDDHA OF DZANGAR RIDES IN A MULE LITTER

Lakatsang is accompanied by his steward, some monks, and a boy Buddha. The photograph was made in the grass lands below Kemar Pass, at an elevation of 12,400 feet.

old town of Taochow. From there to Labrang 34 mules carried our loads. At this influential monastery we spent nearly a week making plans to cross the grass lands on our way to the Amnyi Machen.

I engaged 20 armed and mounted men of the nomad Sokwo Arik tribe of Mongol origin to escort us and to supply 60 big yaks. We had also to buy yak-hair hobbles for the horses. These were used in the daytime, when the horses grazed. At night, to keep thieves from driving them off, we had to hobble them with locked irons.

LABRANG, ONE OF THE LARGEST MONASTERIES IN EASTERN TIBET

These days at Labrang taught me much of this bleak, dusty, religious stronghold, 8,585 feet above the sea. To-day nearly 5,000 lamas live in this huge monastery. Its site, once a great marsh, was changed into dry land by the prayers of a former Buddha, I was told (see pages 136, 137).

On a hillside opposite the monastery grows a forest of fir and spruce. It is of miraculous origin, says tradition. Long ago a famous monk, the founder of Labrang, got a haircut. His hair, scattered over the hillside, took root and produced this fine forest!

There are 30 large buildings in Labrang which contain chanting halls or which serve as the homes of Living Buddhas. Many hundreds of smaller buildings house the lamas. With their great wooden shutters, the houses look like jails.

Some of these structures are from four to five stories high. Some are red; others are yellow with green roofs. All seem very old. On a hillside, towering above all others, stands the residence and private chapel of the chief Buddha. Its roof is covered with gold sheets, or probably with bronze sheets over which gold has been plated (see page 135).

Five giant kettles, each six feet in diameter, equip a monster kitchen. Here food sufficient to feed 4,000 lamas can be boiled at one time. It usually consists of butter tea or rice gruel.

Amazing is the main chanting hall, which seats 4,000 persons. One hundred forty red columns, 40 feet long, support its roof. In another hall, preserved in massive silver urns, are the remains of the four previous incarnations of a Buddha, the founder of Labrang, who traveled widely in Mongolia and China and gathered much silver used in building this monastery.

The big hall is unclean. After prayers the lamas are fed here, and the floor is thick with tea, rice gruel, and other food dropped there in years gone by and now trampled hard. About the padded strips of carpet on which the lamas sit, this ancient food is many inches thick.

I called on the Abbot in charge. He received us in his room, which was beautifully painted and paneled. On a shelf stood lovely porcelain bowls made during the reign of Kien Lung; others dated back even to Kanghshi. I also saw here handsomely carved silver chests containing gilded or gold images. There were also fine carpets, painted and lacquered tables, and other signs of wealth and plenty.

A TALK WITH THE ABBOT OF LABRANG

I had an extraordinary interview with the Abbot. Among other things, he asked me if I had ever been in a land where the people had the heads of dogs, sheep, and cattle. When I said that such people did not exist, he smiled politely.

"Oh, yes, they do," he said. "Our books tell of such people."

He also asked me what I thought about the shape of the world. He said he believed the earth was flat, and that in its center was a lofty mountain, behind which the sun disappeared and thus produced night. He also said that foreigners had verified the existence of this big mountain by flying over it. His simplicity and childlike credulity were astounding.

Adjoining this monastery is a trading village and the barracks of the Moslem soldiers. Here is incredible filth. Walls are built of sheep and yak bones. The ground is littered with bits of skin, legs, hoofs, and the bones of animals. Frozen dogs lie in the middle of the street, and there are dead birds and stagnant pools of blood from slaughtered sheep and yak, as well as entrails, bits of wool, and discarded parts of the slain animals, among which dogs and chickens prowl for food.

I hastened back to my clean quarters.

Outside, the wind howled and drove filth-laden dust across a dreary landscape.

It was now the fifth of May, yet a blizzard raged. At dawn our 60 yaks were driven in by the nomad escorts. Accompanying me was an extraordinary American character, a missionary whom I found working among the people about Choni and engaged as Tibetan interpreter. He was dressed now in nomad garb.

THE EXPEDITION'S TROUBLES ARE NEVER OVER

I could hardly believe that, after the many months of delay, the day of departure was really at hand. But, of course, our troubles were never over. The nomads, familiar only with handling bags and bundles, did not know how to tie our boxes and Army trunks on the yaks, so many a load fell off and had to be tied on again. Soon our caravan was scattered out for a distance of a mile.

Out from Labrang the trail ran up a valley on the left side of the Song Chu stream. Natives ran out to gaze at us as we passed. Out of the Labrang Valley we emerged into the grass lands, or yet another broad valley. Here the fearless Ngura tribe had defeated the Moslems, and the grassy plain was still strewn with the bones of those who fell in that fierce fight (see, also, text, page 141).

Now we had indeed left the world behind. Slowly we made our way over the snow-covered valley of the Song Chu. Beside the loaded yaks the mounted nomads, clad in sheepskins and carrying rifles and their dreaded 30-foot spears, rode along, whistling (see, also, page 136).

Night came and we camped. In each yak's nose is a ring to which is tied a small rope; this, in turn, is tied to a long picket line.

To start their fires the Tibetans used a crude sheepskin bellows. We put out sentries, many of whom had mastiffs with them. Great was the astonishment of the tribe when I played my phonograph and when, for the first time, the "canned" voices of Caruso, Melba, and others were heard in the high grass lands. The altitude of our first camp was 10,250 feet, estimated by boiling point.

I studied these Tibetan nomads. A swarthy, stalwart lot they were, wearing

A MARVEL OF THE SER CHEN GORGE, OR GREAT GOLD VALLEY

The awe-inspiring canyon has been cut by water from the red sandstone. In the walls of the canyon are many caves. A man stands at the edge of the glacier, which is discharging from the cavern in the background. Here junipers grow at 10,400 feet elevation (see, also, text, page 158).

THE LAMASERY OF RADJA, NEAR THE HEADWATERS OF THE YELLOW RIVER

Standing 10,000 feet above the sea, at the base of a 1,500-foot bluff, only about two-thirds of this mysterious lamasery is visible in the photograph (see text, page 159). To the left, at the top of the slope and under the sheer rock wall, are the quarters of hermit monks (see, also, illustration, page 153).

THE AUTHOR'S IMPOSING YAK CARAVAN ASSEMBLED IN THE COURTYARD AT DZANGAR MONASTERY

Ready for the march to Radja, on the Yellow River, the yaks are all loaded. Each pack is guarded against rain by a heavy felt cover. From the roof, a Buddha and his steward enjoy the excitement of the start.

THE YELLOW RIVER, SEEN FROM THE SUMMIT OF AMNYI CHUNGUN,
MOUNTAIN GOD OF RADJA

The highest point of the cliff that overshadows the Radja Lamasery is 11,500 feet above sea level. Black dots to the left of the river are the camp of Hdzanggur Ngoloks (see, also, page 157).

large sheepskin coats with long sleeves. When driving yaks, they slap the animals over the back with these sleeves. As soon as their tea had boiled, they took out a ladleful, put butter in it, then threw it out of their chief's tent, at the same time yelling prayers to the mountain god. They called all foreigners "Urussu," or Russians. My phonograph they called a "Russian magic box."

I slept lightly that night, what with barking dogs and the firing of rifles by our sentries to scare away thieves. In the morning my thermometer stood at 25 degrees Fahrenheit.

These grass lands in summer are veritable bogs. The water-soaked ground reminded me much of some of the summit bogs in the Hawaiian Islands.

At lunch time we let our laden yaks loose to graze. The horses were hobbled with hair ropes, one front leg tied to one hind leg. If ever a man should lose his horse in that wide, open country it might be gone for good, as lassos are unknown.

Near us was an abandoned nomad camp where the Moslems had done their worst, killing hundreds. Now not a soul was visible in the whole wild, dreary region of great bogs and streams of quicksand.

WATCHED BY ROBBER TRIBES

One of my boys was thrown by his horse. It galloped away, empty stirrups flying. Before we could catch it ten armed nomad robbers rushed out from hiding, encircled the horse and drove it off. This made me realize how the Amchok and perhaps other robber tribes were watching us.

For some days we continued over dreary snow-covered or water-soaked land, dark under low-hanging clouds.

The Sokwo Ariks proved a surly escort. One villain, with nose and lips split from many battles, threatened me with his spear simply because I urged him to protect his loads with the usual felt covers

Crossing one of the divides between Labrang and the Yellow River was a physical ordeal. A 50-mile gale blew powdery snow over the ridges and whirlwinds sent white columns spinning high in air. Our figures became hazy white outlines in the blinding storm. With numb fingers I took photographs of the panting yaks floundering like huge snowplows through the pass. At the summit, 13,000 feet up, the wind nearly blew us from our horses. I felt my cheeks freezing.

Descending, we saw in a valley at our right a deserted camp of the nomads. There were old mud stoves and so-called sacrificial altars made of square blocks of yak dung piled about three feet high. Here they burned their sacred offerings of juniper twigs. We paused a while and our yaks pushed away the snow with their noses in a search for bits of grass.

Though the wind still blew, it was now dry, for it came off the Gobi. Crossing on over the Tek Gar Tang plain, we came down to the camp of the Sokwo Ariks on the Mamo Zhung, at an elevation of 11,500 feet. Although they are Tibetans, these tribesmen live in Mongol felt yurts instead of yak-hair tents. Because of their fierce dogs, which attack all strangers, we camped a little below them.

NOMADS LAUGH AT OPERATIC SONGS

We rested here a day and obtained fresh yaks to take us on to Dzangar, a monastery in a ravine not far from the gorges of the Yellow River. It was to Dzangar only that the Sokwo men had agreed to escort us.

The valley about our Mamo Zhung camp fairly swarmed with wild fowl, and I feasted. This amazed the nomads, who consider fowl and eggs unclean. Here again I set up my phonograph. The men roared with laughter at the pathetic songs from "La Bohème" and "Pagliacci." Sitting about, listening to the music, they smoked, lighting their pipes with smoldering yak dung. I bought fuel here, paying for it with needles and thread.

With fresh yaks we resumed our march, going into the Htse Chu Valley. The river has its source not far from the Yellow River. It flows east, bends sharply north, then south and southwest into the Yellow. We forded it at an elevation of 11,250 feet, at the same place where the German traveler, Futterer, coming from the north, crossed it some years ago. In fact, it was Futterer who put the Htse Chu on the map. Later he was robbed by nomads and arrived half-naked at Taochow. On this river we found many ducks and even sea gulls, which apparently summer on the waters of the Koko Nor.

THE CHIEF LIVING BUDDHA OF RADJA LAMASERY

He is considered the incarnation of the mother of Tsongkapa, the founder of the Yellow Reformed Sect of Buddhists, who are called the *Gelugpa,* or Followers of Virtue.

chen Lamas. Then we went, as is the custom there, to take tea with his steward. This sounds quite formal, like polite life in England or America, but a Tibetan tea party is, to say the least, a gastronomic endurance test which no squeamish soul could survive.

In the steward's big tent a mud stove was roaring. From curiosity, many nomads with their wives and children followed us as we went in. They were husky, well-built people. In this raw land only the fittest survive.

Soon an old woman brought out some bowls from a pile of sheep manure, which served for fuel as well as a sideboard. She took some ground-up sheep dung in her hand and scoured the dirty bowls; then she polished them with a filthy rag which hung to her girdle and dragged on the filthier ground when she walked. With her dirt-incrusted hands she poured tea into these bowls and they were passed around. I set down these disagreeable facts only to show in what squalor these nomad Tibetans survive.

A wooden box was now set before us. In it lay dirty lumps of yak butter, covered with old dung dust and other unwholesome things. From this box the fingers of many a nomad had dug before me, and I could see the grooves left in the unpalatable mass by their finger nails.

In another compartment of the box was roasted barley flour, or tsamba, the staple food of the Tibetans. I shrank from either tea or food, but I could not offend

West by southwest from here I saw a conspicuous range with five peaks, the two central peaks being very prominent. I estimated this range to be about 16,000 feet high. Natives call it the Aric Dzo Ngon Ma.

A TIBETAN TEA PARTY

Camping next on the Chonakh River, a tributary of the Htse Chu, I heard of an 81-year-old Buddha living near by in a yurt. It was our policy always in this land, where travelers are regarded with suspicion, to make friends as we went. So I called on the old Buddha and presented him with pictures of the Dalai and Pan-

HERMIT QUARTERS OF THE MONKS OF RADJA MONASTERY

The religious recluses subsist on barley flour in winter and on boiled nettles in summer. Their cells are under the conglomerate cliffs back of Radja Monastery, at an elevation of 10,700 feet (see, also, illustration, page 148, and text, page 160).

A LAMA OF RADJA MONASTERY PRINTS BUDDHAS IN THE WATERS OF THE
YELLOW RIVER

On the undersurface of a board this devout man has fastened five brass molds with rows of
Buddhas in bas-relief, such as are used for making sacred mud bricks. By pulling the board
out and letting it sink again, he was "printing" Buddhas in the water, thus acquiring merit (see,
also, illustration, opposite page, and text, page 162).

these simple people, whose impulses were hospitable; so I whistled up courage enough to raise the tea bowl to my lips and take one tiny sip. Fortunately, the old Buddha at that moment sent word that he was ready to have his picture taken, and I had an excuse to leave the tea party without being rude.

We were glad when, after two more days of riding over a monotonous, rolling grass country, we came to a valley called Gan Mar. Through it a stream flows southeast. Wolves ran along parallel to our track at a safe distance, or sat up on the ridges and watched us as we passed. Herds of antelope appeared, too.

Farther on, many black Tibetan tents of the Tsokhar people dotted the valley. The weather here was most fickle. Nowhere have I ever observed such quick changes. As we passed the Tsokhar tents, the air was balmy, almost sultry. Then suddenly a cold blast hit us and hard snow pellets rattled on our coats. In an hour, it was

warm again. That night we camped at 12,100 feet, on the banks of the Runa.

Beautifully colored partridges and many rabbits and marmots flew or scampered up the ravines for cover next day, as we crossed the high Nyinser Pass. Now the grass lands were behind us; we were definitely in the mountain regions. Rhododendron scrub covered the slopes of ravines and gorges.

MARMOTS WHISTLE AT THE EXPEDITION'S DOG

Our dog chased marmots that day until ready to drop from exhaustion. These creatures, which resemble prairie dogs, would sit erect in front of their burrows and whistle at him. Those near their holes easily escaped him by ducking in; but if they were foolish enough to whistle while away from home on a forage, the dog nabbed them. Usually he was victorious; but now and then he retreated with a howl of pain and disgust, as one of the agile rodents valiantly gave battle and bit him on the lips or nose.

Scores of curious lamas sat on the flat roofs of Dzangar to watch us as we filed in and unloaded our yaks.

Here, having fulfilled their contract, our unruly nomad escort left us. They quit without a word of farewell or the slightest sign of interest in me. Having been paid in advance, they simply dumped all my belongings into the manure that covered the compound and walked off. But I was equally glad to be rid of them.

Next day, while fresh yaks and guides were being obtained, I went south five miles to see the Yellow River. My trail ran down the Gokhub Valley, then over a ridge to another ravine. Down both flow streams which unite and empty in the Yellow. From a high bluff near their confluence I beheld the Yellow River.

BRASS MOLDS USED IN "PRINTING" BUDDHAS IN THE YELLOW RIVER

In the cloth beside him is barley, of which a handful was thrown into the river as an offering to imaginary Buddhas, which he "prints" on the face of the waters (see illustration, opposite page).

THE WHITE MAN'S FIRST VIEW OF THE YELLOW RIVER GORGES

No other white man, since time began, ever stood here and beheld these deep gorges of the Yellow River.

Seven hundred feet below the bluff on which I stood flowed the Yellow River, 10,200 feet above the sea. Spruces, birches, and willows clung to the walls of the gorges.

The only way into the Yellow River gorge at this point is through a narrow valley called the Large Gate. We went down to it. Past its mouth roars the main channel of the great river, forming here a terrific whirlpool.

On the walls of the gorge grow dense groves of spruce. I asked the guide to cut the limbs from the trunk of one, so that I might make a close-up picture. But he objected, saying the mountain god of the place would punish us, for once before men had cut trees here, blood had flowed from the stumps and two Tibetans had been crushed to death by the falling trunks. Plainly, said the Tibetan, the god was displeased.

Dzangar shelters 500 lamas and 15 Living Buddhas. The only object of interest

RADJA LAMASERY, HUDDLED BESIDE THE UPPER REACHES OF THE YELLOW RIVER IN TIBET

The author's compound can be seen at the extreme left, separated from the monastery by a gully.

MONKS CELEBRATING THE FESTIVAL OF THE MOUNTAIN GOD, AMNYI CHUNGUN

On the 11th day of the fourth moon prayers to this patron of Radja are held on the lofty slopes back of the monastery. In the tent more than 350 monks chant to Amnyi Chungun (see, also, illustration, page 150, and text, page 162).

A NGOLOK IMP OF RADJA

With improvised parasol he stalked about the lamasery courtyard.

every crack and ledge. It was not unlike certain Colorado scenery.

After establishing camp, I went down the Great Gold Valley to the point where, narrowing down to a rocky gateway, the Ser Chen joins the Yellow River. Here I climbed up beside the stone gateway and, to my amazement, I saw the mighty stream, some 200 feet below, confined to a gorge no more than 80 yards wide.

Here again my American interpreter and I were the first of our race to look down upon this great river imprisoned in this deep gorge, for it may be said that the whole course of the Yellow River from south of Dzangar to and including the gorges north of Radja were absolutely unexplored and never before had been visited by white men.

It gave me a peculiar feeling in this lonely wilderness to be the first to look upon this mighty river flowing through hitherto unknown gorges. The ravine was choked with fallen timber, roots, tangled underbrush, and broken rocks which had fallen from the heights.

The gorges of the Yellow River at the mouth of Ser Chen Valley are not less than 3,000 feet in depth, but the high peaks forming the gorge were not visible from the point where we stood.

To celebrate this first view of these gorges we killed two eagles as natural-history specimens. They are now in the Museum at Harvard.

Going back to camp, we explored the Gold Valley upstream, or north. It changes to a deep gorge with sheer 1,000-

to me in the dilapidated lamasery was a big painting of the god Amnyi Machen.

With some cotton cloth as "money," I hired a runner to go on to Radja and announce our coming. Then our new guides came with 60 fresh yaks and drew lots for our different pieces of baggage, so there would be no row as to who should carry the heaviest.

A BIT OF COLORADO IN THE GREAT GOLD VALLEY

An extraordinary region opened before us when we reached Ser Chen, or Great Gold Valley, on our way to Radja. Weird sandstone cliffs, castles, and wind-hewn rock towers, where eagles nested, rose about us, and fragrant junipers clung to foot-high sandstone walls. Its floor is densely wooded with enormous century-old junipers. Into the walls of the gorge penetrate deep caves, from whose ceilings hang giant icicles like stalactites. Wild it all is, yet uninhabited; hence peaceful.

Flocks of Tibetan eared pheasants whirred from our path next day, as we marched on over recurring ridges and valleys toward Radja. Our trail at times ran along the rocky banks of the Yellow River. Once we startled a flock of wild blue sheep, with great curved horns. Up a dizzy chasm they fled, making spectacular and unbelievable leaps from one rock shelf to the next. Still talking about the sheep, we rode around a sharp point and there, in the valley of the Yellow River, lay Radja, our base from now on.

From my quarters in the Radja lamasery, I could see the Yellow River, and on to the west the wooded slope of a mountain, and a trail leading into the land of the Ngoloks.

THE YELLOW RIVER GORGE, UPSTREAM FROM THE EDGE OF DAKHSO CANYON

Between these lofty walls, three days' journey northwest of Radja, the mighty stream flows at an elevation of 11,000 feet (see, also, p. 161).

THE RADJA BUDDHA ENJOYS A TIMEPIECE SYMPHONY

I called on the local Buddha, of course. Without the aid of these holy men, no intruder from the outside world could last long among these fanatics. His reception room was a curiosity. From floor to ceiling, clocks and watches of every description and size were ticking away, each keeping its own time regardless of the actual hour. Clocks struck at various intervals—some in unison, others in quick succession. An old-style Swiss cuckoo added its raucous squawks to the chronometric cacophony. I gave him one more watch; also, a pair of snow glasses and an American 20-dollar goldpiece.

My interpreter explained the objects of our march and asked our host to help us. The Buddha said little himself, but instructed his steward to advise us.

The Rimong chief, most powerful of the Ngoloks, would probably rob and murder us, predicted the steward. Only recently this wild tribe had even robbed a Living Buddha, taking from him 40 horses and 400 sheep, as his party went over one of the Ngolok trails.

A YOUNG WOMAN OF THE LHARDI TRIBE PHOTOGRAPHED
IN LABRANG

She wears a lambskin cap and her hair is braided in 108 pigtails, a
holy number (see, also, pages 140 and 179).

with our letters declined the job. In the end, the Buddha found a lama, either more courageous or more foolhardy than the rest, who was willing to act.

Besides our letters, we also sent presents to the chiefs. To get an answer, we figured, would require about two weeks—a foolish hope, we were to learn.

While waiting for an answer from the Ngolok chiefs I had an opportunity to study Radja and the gorges of the Yellow River to the north.

Few in the outside world know that Radja Gomba exists. Life here is unbelievably crude. On the hillside back of the lamasery, for example, are the huts of many hermit lamas, some even from the wild Ngoloks. Ceilings of these huts are so low that a man cannot stand erect in them; yet here these austere creatures spend their years. Others live in caves in the near-by cliffs. Prayer, meditation, and abstinence are their lot. They certainly *do* abstain! In winter they live on barley flour; in summer their chief diet seems to be stewed nettles (see pages 148, 153).

My three letters of introduction to the Ngolok chiefs, given me at Labrang, were of no use, in the local Buddha's opinion. Better not send them at all. Our best plan was to leave our slow yaks at Radja, get on our horses, and make a quick dash for the Amnyi Machen—that is, accomplish our aim before the Ngoloks became aware of our plans.

I demurred. Such a dash would leave me no chance to explore or make pictures. After more argument the Buddha finally changed his mind and said he would send my messages to the Ngolok chiefs, advising them of my approach. At first, every man who was asked to go as a messenger

"THE LIVING BUDDHA BUSINESS IS A POLITICAL SYSTEM"

The Radja Lamasery's drinking water is carried up from the river in huge wooden buckets. I rigged up a filter from kerosene tins to get part of the mud out of the yellow water, which was as thick as pea soup. This amused the lamas and stimulated the loquacity of our good-na-

THE AUTHOR'S CAMP IN DAKHSO CANYON

Set among spruce and willow and viewed from a trail leading to Ngarkigongma (a bluff overlooking the Yellow River gorges), this camp stands at 10,146 feet above sea level. Dense woods cling to the northern slopes, but on southern exposures slopes are bare, owing to earlier melting of snows.

tured old water-carrier. Not being a native of the place, he commented freely on the habits of the lamas at Radja.

The Living Buddha business, he said, was a political or diplomatic system and always worked out for the good of the rich and influential. The local Buddha was very rich; so was his steward; and when "reincarnations" occurred, it seemed to him that this "miracle" always happened just as it might have been desired by the chief Buddha. For example, when the daughter of a powerful chief died, she was soon afterward incarnated in the person of a small boy, a nephew of the Buddha's

steward—a business and political arrangement agreeable to all concerned! When one of the minor Buddhas of Radja died he, too, was happily, conveniently, and quickly reincarnated, this time in the person of the steward's brother!

I smiled and asked the water-carrier how it happened that none of his children was the reincarnation of some departed Buddha. With a twinkle in his eye, he remarked that it was because the sum of all his worldly goods was two goats.

There is no such thing as a jail in Radja, we were told. Lamas who steal, or break other important laws, are tied

THE BUTSANG NGOLOK CHIEF AND HIS WIFE

The daughter of the King of the Ngawa tribe appears in all her finery.

the passing river. By doing so, he acquired merit. He occupied himself in this way for hours (see pp. 154-5).

I was invited by the chief Buddha to a picnic to celebrate t h e feast of Amnyi Chungun, the mountain god of Radja. My host rode ahead on a horse, followed by about five hundred lamas. They went up on the mountain, set up their tents, and improvised an altar whereon offerings of juniper twigs were burnt. Between prayers they ate all the usual unpalatable Tibetan delicacies a n d drank their strong tea from dirty cups.

After final prayers the Buddha left, riding a beautiful horse with i t s saddlecloth and trappings of gold brocade and sheltered by a big gilded umbrella. When he was safely out of sight, the lamas played hilarious games and frolicked to their hearts' content in a very childish manner.

up and beaten; then, with duncecaps on their heads and strings of bones around their necks, and brooms in their girdles, they are driven from the monastery.

PRINTING IMAGES ON WATER

Walking along the river one day, I found a lama who seemed to be playing in the water. He had a board about two feet long with a string tied to it. He would let the board float away a bit, then pull it back. Two hours later when I returned he was still there, playing with that board. On the underside were five brass molds, such as are used in making mud bricks, decorated with numerous images of the Buddha. On investigation I found that he was printing images of the Buddha on

Back in Radja a fair was under way. Many Ngoloks from the Hdzanggur tribe were camped on the Yellow River opposite the lamasery. Here a ferry of inflated goatskins supporting a raft of poles was in operation. These skins soon went flat. After each trip the Tibetans had to blow up each skin—excellent exercise for the lungs. As many as 12 people would ride on one of these flimsy rafts. Horses and cattle, of course, had to swim, and often, as I later learned to my sorrow, working animals are drowned in this swift stream (see, also, page 164).

I crossed over to the Ngolok camp to see what these almost unknown wild people were like. Though very suspicious of us, they showed the greatest curiosity about our appearance and clothing. My interpreter heard o n e of them say: "Till now we have never seen men like you. What are you doing here?"

POCKETS AND BUTTONS AMAZE THE NGOLOKS

They formed a circle about me, feeling my clothes. My pockets in p a r t i c u l a r amused them. "They are casings for the hands," they said. My shoes also aroused admiration and the Ngoloks wondered how so many stitches could be taken in leather. Buttons and buttonholes amused them. T h e y followed me about, shaking their heads in bewilderment.

I pointed my camera at them and tried to explain its use, but they ran away. I did manage to photograph one wild fellow, however. H i s abdomen was c o v e r e d with straight scars, made w h e n h e had held burning rags against his body to cure his stomach ache. These

THE WIFE OF A BUTSANG NGOLOK CHIEF WEARS A GOWN OF GORGEOUS DECORATION

Suspended from her hair is a long strip of red cloth, to which are fastened large opaque, canary-yellow amber beads and long pieces of red coral. Immediately below her hair are rows of turquoise and silver buttons. From each side of her waist hang leather strips decorated with silver and terminating in disks of ivory. The amber is bought at the rate of ten ounces of silver for one ounce of amber, which comes from the Baikal region, in Siberia.

scars were so evenly placed that they looked like tattoo-marks. Other Ngoloks had scars on wrists and hands, marks of fiery ordeals to cure rheumatism (see page 166).

After our arrival at Radja two Moslem traders appeared and bartered for 88 yaks from the Ngoloks. Radja ferrymen, with certain confederates, tried to steal these yaks from the traders. During the night, at their third attempt, the traders fired and killed one of the would-be thieves,

then fled across the river to the lamasery.

Next morning the river bank opposite us looked like a war camp. All the friends and kin of the dead tribesman had gathered to avenge his death. Their first act was to drive away the 88 yaks belonging to the Moslem traders. Others got ready to cross the river to catch the two now frightened traders, who, fearing for their lives, sent over some money, horses, and a rifle as a peace offering to the family of the man they had killed.

SKIN RAFTS ON THE YELLOW RIVER AT RADJA

Such craft consist of from six to twelve inflated goat or sheepskins tied to a few sticks. To cross the swiftly flowing river on one of these rafts is a rather precarious undertaking. Here the author's party has just been ferried across on two rafts tied together (see page 162).

Apparently satisfied with this easy haul of yaks, money, and horses, the tribesmen shouldered their dead comrade and made off.

Although the two Moslems appealed to the chief Buddha, he was powerless. The guilty clan paid not the slightest attention to him; in fact, a few nights later, they stole some of his own horses and sheep.

We heard that one Ngolok raiding party, the winter before our arrival, had crossed the ice on the frozen river, robbed and looted at will, and returned unmolested to its camp.

THE BUDDHA SENDS OUT A "CURSING EXPEDITION"

The Ngoloks are no respecters of persons. One day, while awaiting answers from our messages to them, the Buddha suddenly informed me that we should start at once on our final dash. News had just reached him that a member of his lamasery, returning from the Ngoloks, had been robbed and killed. In punishment the lama council was sending a "curs-ing expedition." Sixty monks were to go to the tribe that had done the killing and put the monastery's official curse on it. By joining this cursing party, the Buddha believed I could easily get into the forbidden country.

I had no qualms about going on a cursing party, but I could not get my yaks ready in time, so I was left behind. Later, I learned the cursees met the cursers halfway and paid indemnity to escape the threatened evil spell. Fearless as the Ngoloks are, they are also very superstitious.

While still waiting for an answer to my letter to the chiefs, I went on a side trip to explore the gorges of the Yellow River. With an old guide from the Gartse tribe and 15 yaks, I followed a trail which crossed at right angles many deep ravines coming down to the Yellow River from its north bank. An odd physiographic feature of these ravines and lateral valleys is that their formation seems reversed. Toward their heads they are often a mile wide and are bare of vegetation;

TRAVELING HDZANGGUR NGOLOKS, ON THE WESTERN BANK OF THE YELLOW
RIVER

Back of the skin bags are two rifles, with the indispensable forks on which the weapons are
rested when discharged (see, also, illustration, page 142).

farther downstream they merge into grass
lands, and at their mouths, where they
debouch into the Yellow River, they are
merely rocky gates a few yards wide.

THROUGH AN EMPTY WORLD

Uphill and down, through canyons and
over passes with odd, gurgling names, we
pushed our toiling way through an empty
world. Not a human being appeared anywhere in that forsaken region.

Then, atop the Mokhur Nira (Pass), at
an elevation of 12,800 feet, I got my first
view of the Amnyi Machen. All I saw,
however, was one dome-shaped mass of
purest white. Far off to the south a long
snow-covered range extended from east to
west. South of it lies Ngolok land.

From the Mokhur Nira we climbed a
peak to the right of the pass, to an elevation of 13,220 feet, from which we gained
a much better view of the Amnyi Machen.
To the north its peaks decrease in height
more rapidly than to the south, the whole
range appearing as one large mountain
mass. It does not extend down the knee

of the Yellow River, as most maps indicate, but is a single mountain mass.

There are several lower ranges east of
the Amnyi Machen more or less parallel
to it. From the Mokhur Pass we now
descended into a narrow, rhododendron-
covered, swampy valley which led into a
canyon, where we spent the night at an
elevation of more than 11,000 feet. The
rock, as in most other places in the Yellow
River gorges, is shale and schist.

From here we climbed to a 11,700-foot
bluff and took photographs west-north-
west of the Yellow River, which flowed
about 2,000 feet below in a terrific gorge,
with vertical walls furrowed by landslides.
Then we descended directly through forest
into Dakhso Canyon, a walk of more than
two days. At the very foot of the trail
is a small grassy space, the only available
camping ground. We spent four days in
Dakhso Canyon, exploring the forests by
following up the stream bed over bowlders
and fallen logs (see pages 159, 161).

On June 2, a morning with a deep blue
sky and cirrus clouds, we climbed to a

A NGOLOK OF THE HDZANGGUR TRIBE IN TIBET

He lives about three days' journey west of the Yellow River from Radja. The tattoolike marks on his abdomen are not there for ornament, but were burnt in with flaming bits of rags to cure indigestion (see text, page 163). Around his neck he wears charms.

chen during the time it would take him to drink a bowl of tea. Any other comparison, such as saying "in 10 or 20 minutes," would have been meaningless to him. He replied, "Yes, I have heard that in foreign countries people can get inside of an eagle and are thus able to fly." He seemed amazed when we told him a machine was used for flying. "But of course you use eagle feathers!" he insisted. It is difficult to explain anything to such simple people, whose only means of transport is the yak, which travels at two miles an hour.

From Dakhso we returned to Radja by another route, through absolute wilderness, primeval forests, and terrific canyons hitherto untrodden by the foot of white men.

Still without word from the Ngolok chiefs, we went on an 18-day trip to explore the Jupar Range. Here, too, we were undoubtedly the first of our race to plant foot. And again, from this region, we could see the towering Amnyi Machen.

Disappointment was ours on our return to Radja. Neither the escorts nor the yaks we had bargained for were ready. In fact, we were bluntly told nobody would go with us. A warning had come from the wild Ngoloks that no one should aid us to get into their country, and the people were afraid.

In despair, I threatened the lamasery people. Unless we were immediately provided with escort and animals I would ask aid of the Sining Moslems, whom they

high bluff, Ngarkigongma, which permitted a magnificent view of the Yellow River gorges. I took several photographs downstream, numerous rapids appearing in the distance. To the north the mountains became higher and the Yellow River gorges consequently deeper.

PRIMITIVE MAN'S CONCEPTION OF AIRPLANES

On the climb to the top of Ngarkigongma we took our nomad yak driver along. As we looked across the peaks and gorges, we remarked to him that with an airplane one could reach the Amnyi Ma-so much feared. This brought the lama council quickly to time.

We could cross the Yellow River at Radja, they advised; go first to the camps of the Tawu clan, and from there it would be only one day to Amnyi Machen. To be able to move quickly in case of attack, we decided to use only horses and take an irreducible minimum of food, tents, and clothes.

The chief of the Radja council said he would send word at once to the Jazza clan's camp, west of the Yellow River, and I agreed to hire the male members of that clan to escort us to the mountain. The lamas, however, could not guarantee our safety, and should the Ngoloks or other robbers attack us they would not be responsible for our lives and property. To this I agreed. I had come to the conclusion that to work at the Amnyi Machen peacefully would be

TWO NGOLOKS OF THE HDZANGGUR TRIBE AT RADJA

The man to the left is in the act of taking snuff, which consists mainly of the ashes of yak dung. In one hand he holds a snuffbox and snuff on the thumb of the other. Photographed in the Ngolok encampment, opposite Radja, on the west bank of the Yellow River, with part of Radja appearing in the background.

out of the question. It is feasible to get there, but to stay and work is another story. It would mean either keeping a large, well-armed party for one's protection or else depending upon the friendly coöperation of all the Ngoloks.

SPIES INFORM NGOLOKS OF THE EXPEDITION'S PLANS

In the meantime, while making preparation for the hazardous journey, some spies informed the Ngoloks of our plans. Most likely it was the ferrymen and the old water-carrier (see pages 160-1). His

brother-in-law (a Butsang Ngolok chief) had already sworn that if ever we should come anywhere near his encampment it would be the end of us. The Radja lamas, too, had warned us not to go. They said the Hdzanggur Ngoloks were waiting for us in the Gur Zhung Valley. One tribesman, in fact, came boldly into our compound and in a bluffing voice said, "You had better not go, for all the Ngoloks are aroused and are awaiting you to rob and perhaps murder you."

Notwithstanding these threats, we laid our plans. The chief of the Jazza clan

A SEA OF MOUNTAINS CULMINATES IN THE PEAKS OF AMNYI MACHEN

A view of bare mountain regions, taken from Woti La (Pass), at an elevation of 14,680 feet. The author was on his way to the Jupar Range, eighteen days' journey from Radja, when this photograph was made.

THE BA VALLEY OF TIBET, FROM ITS SOUTHERN RIM IN THE BA PLAIN; ELEVATION, 10,400 FEET

The willow-lined Ba stream flows through eroded loess and gravel slopes. On the terraces in the valley (center and left) are the only Tibetan villages in this sea of grass. The inhabitants are called "the people living under the ground." The Jupar Range, with its bare southern slopes, is visible above the Ba Plain.

BACK FROM A SUCCESSFUL DUCK HUNT

Two of the author's happy Nashi boys enjoyed a short excursion into the Ba Valley, notorious for its robber tribe, the Shabrang.

what silver he had left from the amount advanced him, as I had decided to return to Labrang. Then we recrossed the Yellow River to Radja and announced that we would return to Labrang.

To give our plan the appearance of truth, I ostentatiously sent two men and our old yak driver to the Gartse tribe to engage cattle to take us to Labrang.

Early the next day Gomba came with 50 taels of silver, and bemoaned the fact that I had given up the journey to the mountain. But I took him aside and told him to keep the money and say nothing. "Fetch the rafts and load them with our belongings," I said. "This very day I shall follow you to your camp and on to the Amnyi Machen, as agreed."

The water-carrier, whom I suspected as a spy, we sent on an errand to the lamasery.

came to discuss terms regarding our trip. We were to make a large encampment in three days, and there engage Kangsar Ngoloks to escort us farther. He also said if we did not stay too long at the Amnyi Machen there would probably be no danger.

July 11 was set for our departure. Gomba, the Jazza chief (see p. 172), came early, but on that morning we had an accident while crossing the Yellow River. One horse was drowned. I pretended to be discouraged and announced that I would either not go at all or else postpone the journey. I had, however, a plan to mislead everyone, even my own entourage. I told Gomba to come next day and bring

We took several horses instead of yaks and loaded them lightly, so as to make quick progress. All had assembled on the river bank. To expedite the crossing, Gomba's tribesmen took off their clothes and stuffed them into goatskins taken from the inflated rafts; then they fastened the skins around their bodies, while each drove a horse into the river and, taking hold of the horse's tail, swam across, or rather let the horse pull him to the other bank.

We assembled our loads and when all was ready followed downstream on the muddy bank to the little valley of Ulan. This we ascended. As we turned into the ravine I beheld an ominous black-blue sky and knew that we were in for a terrific storm. Gomba suggested that we wait until it had passed; so I found shelter in a dry brook bed, under an overhanging ledge of rock. The storm broke, but soon we all went on in spite of rain, lightning, and deafening peals of thunder. The stream bed had become a red torrent, which we had to cross and recross many times, while the steep hillside had become unscalable red-clay mudslides.

Eventually we emerged from the storm at an 11,650-foot pass. From here we had a beautiful view westward over a vast rolling land. We descended into the Sher Lung Valley; thence to a stream which flows in a narrow canyon to the Yellow River. The water was a deep red, but the fording was not difficult. We continued up a lateral valley skirting small ravines, and, after crossing a steep spur, arrived at the encampment of the Jazza clan just in time to pitch our camp before dark.

THE YELLOW CHINESE POPPY OF THE TIBETAN HIGHLANDS

The flowers are often more than six inches across. This specimen of *Meconopsis integrifolia* was photographed in the upper Jupar Valley in July, at an elevation of 12,600 feet.

THE EXPEDITION GOES FORTH INTO THE UNKNOWN

This was the first time any white man had ever camped west of the Yellow River and east of the Amnyi Machen. We were in absolutely unknown territory, unknown from every standpoint. After a sleepless night, owing to the barking of the nomad dogs, we arose, got our escort together, and sallied forth.

Our first objective was Amnyi Druggu, a high mountain facing the snow peaks, from which vantage point we hoped to photograph the Amnyi Machen as a whole. But across the Gur Zhung Valley a still better view can be had than from Amnyi Druggu. The trail led southwest on the bare grassy slopes, with not a tree visible anywhere (see map, page 138).

To our right extended cliffs of purplish-red conglomerate, a continuation of the Radja cliffs, through which the Yellow River has cut its way. These cliffs culminate beyond the Jazza encampment in a high red bluff. This prominent feature of the landscape, crowned by juniper trees, is called Amnyi Geto, the mountain god of the Jazza clan. At its base, on the left

GOMBA, NICKNAMED DADDA, CHIEF OF THE JAZZA CLAN

His tribe braved the threats of the Ngoloks and, in spite of them, took the author's party across the Yellow River to the Amnyi Druggu. The felt hat he wears is typical of the Tibetans who live near Radja; even the lamas, when traveling, wear such hats, but in their case the felt is dyed yellow (see text, page 170).

condition of the ground, which resembled one vast bog.

We were now in the territory of the Yonzhi tribe, which extends to the Cheb Chu and Yellow rivers. Poor as the region east of the Yellow River is in game (except for blue sheep, gazelles, and wolves), game to the west, in the Amnyi Machen mountain system, is most abundant. It is difficult to see what prevents these animals from migrating over the Yellow River to the east, when in winter that stream is one sheet of ice.

At the summit of the pass we espied three big sheep, with horns forming tremendous spirals, which did not extend laterally, but formed one huge frontal spiral reaching nearly to the ground. The nomads call these sheep *nyen*. They are undoubtedly related to the Ovis Poli. The Jazza people told us, and I merely repeat it without comment, that the old rams often die of starvation when their horns grow so big that the animals can no longer reach the grass.

of the trail, is an obo, a pile of sticks and rags and rocks. Here the clan burns its incense offering to Geto. The elevation at the obo is 11,800 feet.

We now went west, still over grassy hills, up and down, at an elevation of more than 12,000 feet; then northwest, leaving to our left a deep valley with sunken terraces, one above the other. Then we went down into Drukh Nang, or Dragon Valley, which leads to another pass, the Drukh Gi Nira, at an elevation of 14,250 feet. It is on the border of the Jazza territory. Ascent and descent were very difficult, because of the water-logged

The whole region between the Yellow River and Amnyi Machen is one great zoölogical garden. Wherever I looked I saw wild animals grazing contentedly. There were various deer, wapiti, and many other animals unknown to me.

In order not to meet too soon with the Yonzhi tribe, we decided to camp below the pass, in a small lateral valley, above juniper forest.

After a peaceful night we descended the Hcha Chen Valley. A few miles below our camp it was filled with magnificent juniper forest. While I stopped to photograph, Gomba and my American interpreter went up a small valley to our right, where the Yonzhi chief had had his encampment. There was, however, no sign of any tent. Nomadlike, they had moved again.

The scenery became more and more beautiful as we descended. The little meadows, clearings in the juniper forest, were full of flowers—blue poppies, yellow primulas, and others—out in all their glory. Where the valley narrows into a defile, we found a trail leading through virgin juniper forest.

PRAYERS HUNG ON TREES

It was a glorious day. From the branches of trees there hung, suspended on yak-hair rope, many mutton shoulder blades inscribed with the sacred formula, "Om mani padme hum." These were hung so low that pass-

HIS CLAN'S CAMPS ARE A DAY'S JOURNEY WEST OF THE YELLOW RIVER FROM RADJA

This follower of Gomba (see illustration, page 172) was one of the author's escorts and was photographed in the juniper forest of the Hcha Chen Valley. Around his neck he wears a rosary and silver charm box. A sort of scalp lock hangs over his left shoulder.

ers-by were bound to touch them and thus, by setting them in motion, say the prayers written on them (see page 175).

After crossing a wooded spur over a steep, hard trail, we descended into a lateral valley forested with spruce on the northern slopes and juniper on the southern. Here we found the tents of the Yonzhi tribe. The people were astonished at sight of our party. They joked with Gomba, and one asked, "Why this array of arms and force when visiting our territory?"

We continued up the valley to the very foot of Amnyi Druggu, the mountain god of the Yonzhi tribe. The last few tents we passed were cursed by some plague, the nomads said. The inmates lay dying outside, covered with yak-hair rugs.

Gomba pulled me aside and motioned me not to breathe while passing the dying nomads. He gave them a wide berth. I assumed it was relapsing fever and doubted that it was due to plague.

We pitched camp at 12,500 feet elevation, at the foot of the trail which led to Amnyi Druggu. As we had arrived early in the afternoon, I decided to climb the

A NASHI BOY WITH THE HEAD OF A BLUE SHEEP

These rare animals are found among the cliffs and gorges of the
Yellow River in the vicinity of Radja (see page 159).

of alpines of various species, mainly umbellifers, Parnassia, anemones, Pedicularis, blue and red poppies (*Meconopsis*), legumes, and many Compositæ.

We lingered a considerable time at the summit, enjoying the beauty of a setting sun over the huge mass of the Amnyi Machen.

THE GLORY OF THE AMNYI MACHEN

Next morning we climbed again to the summit of Amnyi Druggu, which is in the very center of a spur facing the snowy peaks. Before us lay, in all its whiteness and purity, the glory of Amnyi Machen. Not a cloud was in the sky. We could photograph to our heart's content. I also took pictures looking east over the deep depression in which flowed the Yellow River, and north toward the Jupar Range, which we had previously explored (see text, page 166). Below us, in the valleys, camped the Ngoloks, apparently unaware of our presence.

While on the peak I observed a nomad climbing Amnyi Druggu from the west. Our presence did not disturb him in the least. He came to pay his devotion to the god Amnyi Machen by lighting juniper branches near an obo (see pages 171-2). He knelt down and bowed deeply three times toward the peaks, his forehead touching the ground.

From our camp at the foot of Amnyi Druggu we made excursions to the gorges of the Yellow River, photographing up and downstream from a bluff 1,500 feet above the river. We could see plainly

mountain for the view. It was a stiff job, after a hard day's ride, but we reached the top. Prayer flags decorated the summit, which we determined to be 14,450 feet.

Amnyi Machen's peaks were hidden in clouds. We had only occasional glimpses of the vast snow fields; yet the scenery was superb. In front lay the valley of the Cheb Chu, which joins the Yellow River below Hcha Chen Valley. To the left a deep valley denoted the Yonkokh; to the right was the Yikokh, which with the Domkokh forms the Cheb Chu Valley. I saw no trees whatsoever higher up toward the Amnyi Machen. The ranges were bare, rocky scree or grass-covered. The vegetation on Mount Druggu consisted only

Ngarkigongma above Dakhso Canyon, whence we had photographed downstream (see text, page 166). The Yellow River, flowing here in bare canyons, describes long gentle curves as one looks south, but to the northwest the river can be seen only for a short distance, because of the steepness of the canyon and its sharp turns.

We retraced our steps up the Hcha Chen Valley, camping for the night in the juniper forest. Our nomads made themselves comfortable in a shallow cave. To do some hunting, we ascended farther up the Hcha Chen, to the mouth of a lateral valley.

ONLY TWO SEASONS— SUMMER AND WINTER

From a botanical, or rather dendrological, standpoint, the region was disappointing. The altitudes were too high to permit tree growth. Even the valley floors around the Amnyi Machen reach a height of more than 15,000 feet.

Of alpine plants we found many species; but the flora is not nearly so rich as that farther south. It must be remembered that here there is neither spring nor autumn; only summer and winter—and summer is short. Even in July, snowstorms are not uncommon. The ice in the stream beds of the valleys around Amnyi Machen apparently never melts completely; on our journey in the latter part of July, we found ice three feet thick in many places. All this naturally has its effect on the flora of the region.

MUTTON SHOULDER BLADES ARE TIED TO A YAK-HAIR ROPE AND FASTENED TO BRANCHES OF TREES, USUALLY OVER A TRAIL

These bones are inscribed with the sacred formula, "Om mani padme hum." As they are suspended over the path, the traveler is bound to push them aside when passing; and when he sets them in motion he says all the prayers written on them for the good of the party who hung them up.

One of the handsomest alpine plants we saw was a large pink to mauve and blue-flowered crucifer of a most delicate fragrance, suggestive of vanilla. There were apparently two species. They grew on alpine meadows as well as among rocks, but never lower than 13,000 feet.

In the upper Hcha Chen we literally ran into wapiti, deer, and musk deer. While the men went hunting, I climbed to a rocky peak above our camp and obtained a glorious view, especially of the great pyramid of the Amnyi Machen, the base of which

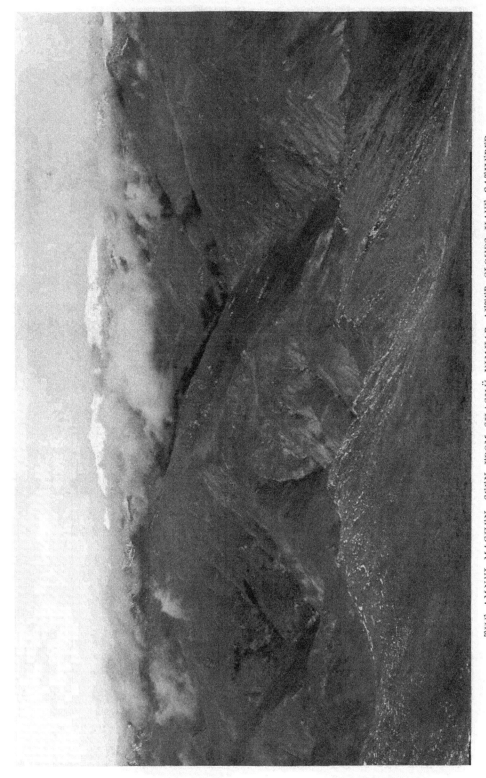

THE AMNYI MACHEN, SEEN FROM SHACHÜ YIMKAR AFTER CLOUDS HAVE GATHERED

"I shouted for joy as I beheld the majestic peaks of one of the grandest mountain ranges of all Asia." The central snow-capped peak towers to a height of more than 28,000 feet (see text, page 185).

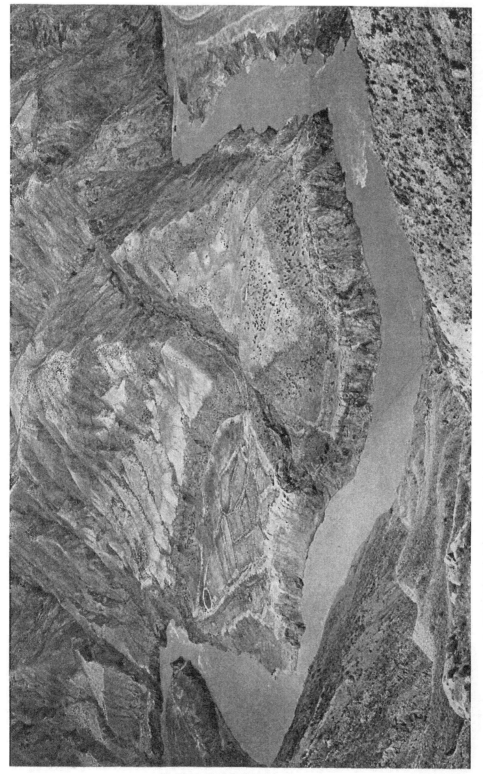

A HORSESHOE BEND IN THE YELLOW RIVER NEAR THE MOUTH OF THE JUPAR NANG

The rocks forming the river bank are of a deep grayish-blue color.

A CAMP OF THE RUNGWO NOMADS IN THE GRASS LANDS, ON THE BANKS OF THE HTSE CHU, AT AN ELEVATION OF 12,050 FEET

The tents are arranged in a circle and sheep, yaks, and horses are herded overnight in the center of the camp. Tibetan mastiffs are kept among the tents to warn the camp of approaching robbers. It is early morn and the sheep are being led out to graze. In the distance is a large white tent, which marks the camp of a living Buddha who prays for the nomads.

A GROUP OF TIBETAN NOMADS, WITH THEIR YAK-HAIR TENTS, SHEEP, AND PONIES, IN THE GRASS LANDS EAST OF THE KOKO NOR

Most of the women of this family braid their hair in 108 tiny pigtails (see, also, pages 140, 160, and 183). They are richly dressed, to the envy of women whose men own fewer flocks of sheep. These nomads stared in wonder at the white visitor's tables, chairs, and tents—marvels they had never seen before.

MAKING CAMP ON THE GRASS LANDS AT AN ELEVATION OF 11,800 FEET

On the return from the Amnyi Machen adventure, the author and his party pitched their tents on this plain prior to negotiating the 13,400-foot Wanchen Nira (Pass).

A TEA CARAVAN HALTED IN THE SONG CHU GRASS LANDS WEST OF LABRANG

The caravan consisted of 800 yaks and had been 20 days en route from Sungpan, in northwest Szechwan. The tea, of the poorest grade, was composed of large leaves and twigs. It was grown in the Min River Valley, near Kwanhsien, in Szechwan, ten days south of Sungpan. In Kwanhsien this tea sells for $3.00 a bale of 120 pounds, but in the grass lands the price goes to $30 and $40 a bale.

THE TENTS OF A NOMAD TRIBE ARRANGED IN A CIRCLE

The author encountered this summer camp four days' journey east of Radja, on his return journey to Labrang.

MAKING CAMP IN HIGH ALTITUDES CALLED FOR MAXIMUM PHYSICAL FORTITUDE AND POWERS OF ENDURANCE

The last of the author's caravan of 60 yaks reaches the Sokwo Arik nomad encampment, at an elevation of 11,450 feet, in the grass lands west of Labrang.

A NOMAD WOMAN OF THE KOKO NOR REGION

She wears her hair in 108 plaits in honor of the 108 volumes of the Tibetan classic, the Kandjur (see "Life Among the Lamas of Choni," by Joseph F. Rock, in the NATIONAL GEOGRAPHIC MAGAZINE for November, 1928).

HER ORNAMENTS ARE SUPPORTED BY HER 108 PIGTAILS

Most of the decorations of a Tibetan nomad woman are worn on her back. The bowllike pieces of silver are fastened to strips of red cloth. The picture was taken en route to Rako, in the grass lands east of the Koko Nor.

THE GOD AMNYI MACHEN, AS TIBETANS CONCEIVE HIM TO BE

This painting, in the vestibule of the chanting hall in Atuntze Monastery, northwest Yünnan, represents the god on a white horse. Since he dwells in the snow peaks, those in the background represent the Amnyi Machen Range, with a sun and rainbow (left) and a moon (right). Below him is the Goddess of Springs, with snakes in her hair, on a dragon. The woman riding a deer on a cloud (upper right) is the god's wife. Below her is a guardian god of Amnyi Machen, who is supposed to ride a cow. From top to bottom, on the left, are two lamas; a god known as Tangla and usually pictured as riding a dragon; the god Dontram, on a tiger, and below him the Stone-Mountain god, Tsan. All Tibetans worship Amnyi Machen; every monastery has either a picture or image of him. *Amnyi* means "old man" and corresponds to our "saint." *Ma* means "peacock" and *chen* "great."

was shrouded in billowy clouds. To linger was impossible, as a storm threatened. I descended rapidly to camp, arriving just as the storm broke. When I awoke the next morning, the whole landscape had undergone a change. Not a vestige of green was visible. All lay buried in a deep mantle of snow.

Clouds were hanging heavily over the grass and the spurs around us. We broke camp early. The Tibetans had slept outside without a tent or shelter, save their felt coats, in which they rolled up like cats. Yet they were cheerful and happy, as if they had slept in feather beds. When their tea was ready, one man would take a large ladle, dip it into the pot, and, amid the chanting of prayers, throw the tea into the air as an offering to the mountain gods. Then all would squat down and eat their frugal meal of tea, butter, and barley flour.

From our Hcha Chen Valley camp we climbed the opposite valley wall, deeply covered with snow. Red and blue poppies, bright, fresh, and unharmed, looked happily out of their bed of snow They are as hardy as the people of this region.

The higher we climbed, the boggier became the ground We crossed a ridge at 14,100 feet elevation as the clouds began to disappear in spots, and the sun peeped faintly through the mist, necessitating snow glasses as protection against snow blindness. We found ourselves now in the Tarang Valley. Here the boys went hunting, and brought back a male musk deer, a broiled steak of which was a welcome addition to our scanty bill of fare.

Early the following day we decided to climb Shachu Yimkar in order to obtain still better views of the Amnyi Machen. The gods again were favorable to us, for the snowstorm had cleared the atmosphere and a cloudless sky greeted us. The slopes and the summit of Shachu Yimkar were a sea of loose slate. Tiny rosettes of Saussureas, with woolly heads resembling a drum major's shako, grew among the slate slabs.

I shouted for joy as I beheld the majestic peaks of one of the grandest mountain ranges of all Asia. We stood at an elevation of nearly 16,000 feet, yet in the distance rose still higher peaks—yet another 12,000 feet of snow and ice! Undoubtedly the dome Drandel Rung Shukh is the highest part, although the great pyramid Shenrezig is a close second and more imposing. The third in size and the central peak is Amnyi Machen, whence the range derives its name In it the Tibetans believe Amnyi Machen resides. Not being supplied with a theodolite, I could not take the actual height; but from other observations I came to the conclusion that the Amnyi Machen towers more than 28,000 feet (see page 176).

(see page 176).

With difficulty I tore myself from that sublime view—a view of the eastern massif of the mountain from west of the Yellow River which no other foreigners had ever had. I remained for some time alone on that isolated summit, lost in reverie and easily comprehending why the Tibetans should worship these snowy peaks as emblems of purity.

As this issue of the NATIONAL GEOGRAPHIC MAGAZINE goes to press, a letter, seven weeks in transit, comes from Dr Rock, announcing his safe arrival in Likiang, Yunnan Povince, China, after a thrilling escape from Yungning, where his party had been imperiled by bandits for many days. Retiring by stealth from Yungning, Dr. Rock describes how he and his followers crossed the Yangtze: "It took us two days to make the crossing with the assistance of 22 natives, who worked like Trojans from early morning until after sunset, stark naked, each with only an inflated goatskin tied to his stomach. They would plunge into the rushing river and push us across, as we each sat upon two inflated goatskins. Three men would pull and two would push, and yet we were carried downstream for more than a mile. As we came in contact with a whirlpool we were spun about as on a merry-go-round. All the natural-color photographic plates, cameras, trunks, botanical and ornithological specimens, and the mules and horses of our caravan were finally set across, with the loss of but one mule."

It is hoped that Dr. Rock, having completed his three years of exploration along the China-Tibet border for the National Geographic Society, will be able to return to America late this spring. Accounts of his experiences and of his notable photographic surveys of mountains hitherto unknown to the outside world will appear in subsequent issues of the NATIONAL GEOGRAPHIC MAGAZINE

THE EDITOR.

Photograph by W. Robert Moore

ALMOST EVERY SORT OF PRODUCE FLOODS THE MARKET

Nature is bountiful in Sumatra, and the rich soil yields abundantly of virtually anything that is planted. The shopper at Fort de Kock has a bewildering variety of fruits and vegetables from which to choose (see text, page 194).